MW00532300

HONEST
FAITH

Register This New Book

Benefits of Registering*

- ✓ FREE **replacements** of lost or damaged books

- ✓ FREE **audiobook** – *Pilgrim's Progress,*
  audiobook edition

- ✓ FREE information about new titles
  and other **freebies**

www.anekopress.com/new-book-registration

*See our website for requirements and limitations.

HONEST FAITH

OR, THE CLUE OF THE MAZE

CHARLES H. SPURGEON

We love hearing from our readers. Please contact
us at www.anekopress.com/questions-comments
with any questions, comments, or suggestions.

Honest Faith – Charles H. Spurgeon
Revised Edition Copyright © 2019
First edition published 1892

Cover Design: J. Martin
Editors: Sheila Wilkinson and Ruth Clark

Printed in the United States of America

Aneko Press

www.anekopress.com

Aneko Press, Life Sentence Publishing, and our logos are trademarks of
Life Sentence Publishing, Inc.
203 E. Birch Street
P.O. Box 652
Abbotsford, WI 54405

RELIGION / Christian Life / Spiritual Growth

Paperback ISBN: 978-1-62245-625-3

eBook ISBN: 978-1-62245-626-0

10 9 8 7 6 5 4 3 2 1

Available where books are sold

Contents

Preface

Doubt dims and chills the day. A fog is over all things, and men move about like Egypt's ancients when they *felt* the darkness. Oh, that this mist would lift! The best we can hope for is that the present gloom may pass away speedily and that the cloud may leave a dew behind to nourish a more intelligent and unquestioning faith.

The paragraphs of this little book are not supposed to be an argument. It was not my aim to convince an opponent but to assist a friend. How I have personally threaded the labyrinth of life thus far may be of helpful interest to some other soul who is in a maze. I hope that these pages will assist some true heart to say "he fought his doubts and gather'd strength."[1] Let no man's heart fail him, for the prevalent skepticisms are but "spectres of the mind."[2] Face them, and they fly.

---

1   Alfred, Lord Tennyson, *In Memoriam A. H. H. OBIIT MDCCCXXXIII: 96.*
2   Ibid.

A great poet let fall the expression "honest doubt."[3] How greedily it was clutched at! Modern unbelief is so short of the quality that it seized the label, and in season and out of season, it has advertised itself as HONEST doubt. It was in dire need of a character.

Feeble as our voice may be, we lift it on behalf of *honest faith*.

---

3   Ibid.

Honest Faith

Let Us Live

The most important part of human life is not its end but its beginning. The day of our death is the child of the past, but our opening years produce the future. At the last hour men summon to their bedside a solemnness of thought that arrives too late for any practical result. The hush, and awe, and faraway look, so frequent in departing moments, should have come much sooner. Remember the Hebrew king who fasted and wore sackcloth, while the child was yet alive. *David therefore besought God for the child; and David fasted and went in, and lay all night upon the earth* (2 Samuel 12:16).

But he wisely foresaw the uselessness of lamenting when the scene closed. *Then David arose from the earth and washed and anointed himself and changed his clothes and came into the house of the LORD and worshipped. Then he came to his own house; and when he asked, they set bread before him, and he ate* (2 Samuel 12:20). When asked about his behavior, he said, *Can I bring him back again?* – one of the most sensible questions (2 Samuel 12:23).

It may be a serious business to take the cold iron from the anvil; it seems to us far sadder to stand still and see the hot bar grow cold. Brother, at my side, whoever you may be, let us strike.

How Shall We Live?

With what hammer shall we strike? Ah, there's the rub. Not that it is a question to me personally, but desiring to be a true brother to you, my reader, I word it so for your sake. In fellowship with you, I look around the workshop. Here are hammers – light, bright, and many. See the trademark – *Certified brand-new.* The old smith over yonder says he knows nothing about them. They were left here by a new firm that is always inventing fine things. "At least," says he, "they call themselves a new firm, but I believe they might better be called the long firm: they trade under new names, but they are old rogues." The smith swings a hammer high overhead with a brawny arm and makes the sparks fly and the iron yield. "There," says he, "the old hammer suits me best." You see, good friend, he is only a blacksmith and knows no better. Some people are unreasonably fond of old things. Are these mental Tories any more foolish than those who are fascinated by novelties? We think not.

The old hammer in our forge is faith in God.

Faith Has Wrought Wonders

Faith is a great worker. The men of strong convictions fashion the world upon their anvils. Confidence girds a man's loins and emboldens him to put forth all his energy. In the eleventh chapter of his epistle to the Hebrews, Paul brings forth an honor roll of faith's heroes and erects an *Arc de Triomphe* (arch to celebrate a victory) to their memory. The names stand out in capitals of light: Abel, Enoch, Noah, Abraham; and the sculptured scenes are such as these – *subdued kingdoms, stopped the mouths of lions, quenched the violence of fire* (Hebrews 11:33-34). If the eulogist of faith comes to a pause, it is not because evidence fails him; but he exclaims, *And what shall I more say? For the time would fail me to tell of Gedeon and of Barak and of Samson and of Jephthae, of David also and Samuel and of the prophets* (Hebrews 11:32).

What Has Doubt Achieved?

How is it that no such trophy has ever been raised to the honor of unbelief?

Will the poet of infidelity and the historian of skepticism yet appear? If so, what will their record be? *Wrought righteousness, obtained promises* are not products of doubt (Hebrews 11:33). Doubt is not likely to endure much suffering to *obtain a better resurrection*, for it sneers at the mention of such a thing; the eulogist of doubt would have to be content with lower achievements. But what would they be? What hospitals or orphanages has doubt erected? What missions to cannibal tribes has infidelity sustained? What fallen women or profligate men has skepticism reclaimed and recreated?

> Sing, muse! If such a theme, so dark, so wrong,
> May find a muse to grace it with a song.

The Milton of this subject may turn out to be like the one Gray describes in his *Elegy* as mute and inglorious.[4] *Ye shall know them by their fruits* (Matthew 7:16). What are the precious results of modern thought, which is the alias for new-fashioned unbelief? We hear the shouts of the craftsmen as they repeat their cry, *Great is Diana of the Ephesians* (Acts 19:28). But where are the holy and happy results of the advanced criticism that is so busily undermining the foundations of faith?

Doubt Is Sterile

The fact is that doubt is negative, destructive, and sterile. It inhibits man to nobler things and fails to create hopes and aspirations in the human mind. It is by no means a principle upon which to base life's fabric, for whatever force it has is subversive and not constructive. A principle that tends to nothing but universal smash is not one to which an ordinary man may contentedly commit the ruling of his life.

What if some religious notions are mere fancy, impractical, and imaginary? It is no great thing after all to be good at breaking up the ornaments of the house.

---

4   Thomas Gray, *Elegy Written in a Country Churchyard* (J. Van Voorst, 1834).

However much the coldly wise may rejoice to be rid of what they call rubbish, it will be no great feat to sweep away all the frail fabrics; the genius required is similar to that which is embodied in a monkey or a wild bull.

Our ambition lies in a higher region; we would construct rather than destroy. Since we aspire to honorable and useful lives, we seek a positive force that will bear us onward and upward. Those who prefer to do so may doubt, and doubt, and doubt to the dregs of nothing, but our choice is to find truth and believe it – that it may be a life force to us. No devotee has yet had the audacity to preach a doctrine of "doubt and live," for to manifestly doubt is akin to death; but "believe and live" is the essence of the message from heaven, and we accept it.

Self-Reliance and a Better Reliance

Self-reliance is taught as a moral virtue, and in a certain sense with due surroundings, it is so. Observation and experience show that it is a considerable force in the world. He who questions his own powers and does not know his own mind hesitates, trembles, falters, and fails; his lack of confidence is the author of his disappointment. The self-reliant individual hopes, considers, plans, resolves, endeavors, perseveres, and succeeds; his assurance of victory is one leading cause of his triumph.

A man believes in his own ability, and unless he is altogether a piece of emptiness, he gradually convinces others that his assessment is correct. Even immodest self-conceit has sometimes acted forcefully, just as Dutch courage has supplied the place of valor. The essence of the matter is that confidence of some sort is an item of great importance in accomplishing our objectives, and distrust or doubt is a source of weakness in any and every case. We choose faith then, rather than doubt, as the mainspring of our life. *It is better to wait upon the LORD than to wait upon man* (Psalm 118:8).

Reliance on God – Our Chosen Life Principle

Now if self-reliance can make a man, how much more can God-reliance! This latter choice is more justifiable, more humble, more sure, and more praiseworthy. Our own powers can only reach so far and no further; we are all tethered and unable to go beyond our limit. But the divine power is unlimited and unchangeable; therefore, he who makes it his trust has a force at his back incomparably beyond all others. For all ends which he may wisely pursue, man will have no need to calculate his strength; he may draw upon All-sufficiency. *My help comes from the LORD, who made the heavens and earth* (Psalm 121:2). The greatest Power must in all emergencies prove great enough for us. Because that power is immutable, we may depend upon it as long as eternity endures. It is no small advantage to place our reliance where it may increase from day to day without hazard of excessive confidence.

Divine power is unlimited and unchangeable

This Reliance Works for Good

The moral results of trust in God are admirable. Setting out in life with a sincere and unaffected reliance upon God, a man's success will not make him vain, for he will give the honor to him in whom he trusted. If such a man sustained an entire defeat while depending upon the divine arm, he need not be crushed by the disaster. His failure would involve more dishonor upon God than upon himself. It would be an exalted fate to perish from too great a faith in God. It is clear that whether one succeeds or fails, the influence of faith in the living God is beneficial.

As to whether or not faith in God will produce for us that which is most worth living for, we must each one prove for himself. The probabilities all look that way. It is reasonable that a man trusting in his Maker should benefit by his faith. Some of us are so assured of the excellence of faith from our many joyful experiences that we are content to turn all the future risks of an experiment in our own case upon the largest scale. We deliberately say, *My soul, rest thou only in God, for my hope is from him* (Psalm 62:5).

Skepticism — No Great Achievement

It has been said, "Nothing is easier than to doubt. A man of moderate ability or learning can doubt more than the wisest men believe." Faith demands knowledge, for it is an intelligent grace, able and anxious to justify itself; but infidelity is not required to give a reason for the doubt that is in it. A defiant demeanor and a blustering tone answer its purpose quite as well as argument. In fact, the present trend of unbelief is to know nothing, and what is this but the epitome of ignorance?

Great is the glory of knowing nothing! But God said, *My people were cut off because they lacked wisdom; because thou hast rejected wisdom, I will cast thee out of the priesthood; seeing thou hast forgotten the law of thy God, I will also forget thy sons* (Hosea 4:6).

A man may glide into agnosticism insensibly and remain in it languidly, but to believe is to be alive – alive to conflict and watchfulness. Those who think faith is a childish business will have to make considerable advances towards manliness before they are able to test their own theory.

> Shall we prefer doubt because it is so readily available, or shall we become truth-seekers even if we have to dive like pearl-fishers?

Shall we prefer doubt because it is so readily available, or shall we become truth-seekers even if we have to dive like pearl-fishers? That depends upon our mindset. We shall select our life rule according to the spirit within us. A brave soul will not tamely follow the ignoble way of the many but will aspire to the higher paths even if they are more difficult.

Faith in the Unseen

That we should limit our confidence to the region of our senses is an absurd supposition. *Faith, therefore, is the substance of things waited for, the evidence of things not seen* (Hebrews 11:1). No man has seen, or heard, or tasted the greatest of known forces. Steam, electricity, gravitation, and the rest of the giants are all invisible. The earth is preserved in its orbit by forces which we cannot grasp. *He . . . hangeth the earth upon nothing* (Job 26:7). The visible powers are of minor rank; the more completely a force can be understood by human thought, the more insignificant it is.

Take an illustration from daily life: the old Latin proverb says that it is the mark of a poor man if he can count his flocks. The few pounds which he has saved can be handled by the artisan every hour of the day if their jingle pleases him; but the great banker has never seen his millions, and the evidence that he possesses them lies in certain bonds and bills in which he places unquestionable reliance. He is rich by faith. He could hardly be very rich and actually see his wealth.

For a great life a man must trust a great force, and that force must be to a large extent unseen and beyond ordinary comprehension.

This surely can be no difficulty to a reasonable man. If we must inevitably depend in some circumstances upon forces beyond our sight, why should we not in all circumstances rest ourselves upon the eternal God, though he is and must be invisible? The practice of trusting in a higher power will prove to be elevating and help to raise us above the dull level of materialism. Won't the habit that is pursued in life be the best possible preparation for death, which so many assume is a pilgrimage to a dark and unknown land? Is the blind man as well off in the darkness as those who have their eyes? No, his habit of finding his way in the dark makes him the better off.

If, therefore, faith teaches us to go where sight fails, we shall be the more ready for that region that the mortal eye has not seen. This much is certain – if we follow God by faith, we need not be distressed because of his apparent absence and his actual invisibility. As the dog that hunts by scent doesn't need to see its game, so is he who follows in the way of obedience by faith. He doesn't need to seek signs and tokens, for his faith supplies him with a more certain sense. *We look not at the things which are seen, but at the things which are not seen, for the things which are seen are temporal, but the things which are not seen are eternal* (2 Corinthians 4:18).

God Can Be Known

It has been asserted by some that God cannot be known. Those who say this declare that they know nothing but observable facts, and therefore they are bound to admit that they do not themselves know that God cannot be known. Since they confess to know nothing about it, they should not be offended if we leave them out of our consideration.

He who made the world is certainly an intelligent being – in fact, the highest intelligence; for in myriads of ways his works display the presence of profound thought and knowledge. *Because that which is known of God is manifest to them; for God has showed it unto them. For the invisible things of him, his eternal power and divinity, are clearly understood by the creation of the world and by the things that are made so that there is no excuse* (Romans 1:19-20).

Lord Bacon said, "I had rather believe all the fables of the Talmud and the Koran than that this universal frame is without a mind." This being so, we do in fact know God in such a measure that we are prepared to trust him. He who made all things is more truly an object of confidence than all the things that he has made.

> Who by the closest search can discover the faintest trace of a reason why we should not rely upon the living God?

It would be a strange mind that did not make itself known – as strange as fire that did not burn and light that did not shine. We should find it hard to believe in the eternal, solitary confinement of the Being who made the worlds.

Faith in God Permitted

May a man trust in God? There is another question that answers both itself and this: Wherefore should not a creature trust its Creator? What is to forbid it? Such confidence must be honorable both to the man and to his Maker; it is according to the need of the one and the nature of the other. Who by the closest search can discover the faintest trace of a reason why we should not rely upon the living God?

God's Existence Not Taken for Granted

Do we take God's existence for granted? Certainly not. We believe it to be a fact proved beyond any other. To the candid mind, not diseased with criticism but honestly rational, the existence of a work proves the existence of a worker, a design necessitates a designer, a forethought involves a forethinker. Now, if we were in a desert with Scottish explorer Mungo Park, a bit of moss would be argument enough that God was there. Or for that matter, the sand under our feet and the sun above our heads would suffice to prove that fact. But dwelling on a fair island, teeming with all manner of life, we may count as many proofs of the Godhead as there are objects of sight, and hearing, and taste, and smell.

This, of course, is called a mere platitude, but by the gentleman's leave, his Latin word makes no difference to the absolute certainty of the argument.

If more proofs were offered, they would no doubt be blocked in the same faultfinding manner, but contemptuous expressions are no replies to fair reasoning. We conceive that one sound proof is better than twenty faulty ones, and if that one does not convince, neither would a legion.

The French savants, en route for Egypt, pestered Napoleon with their denials of a God, but his astute intellect was not led astray. He took them upon deck, and pointing to the stars he demanded, "Who made all these?"

> *The heavens declare the glory of God; and*
> *the firmament shows the work of his hands.*

One day provides a word for the next day,
and one night declares wisdom unto the
next day. There is no speech nor language,
where their voice is not heard. (Psalm 19:1-3)

Doubt Logically Carried Out

Doubt as to the being of God has but a short way to
run to finish its legitimate career. No man who believes
that he has a soul can give better proof
of his mental being than that which we **God's works**
can give of the existence of God. Let **demonstrate**
him try. He claims that his own con- **that he is.**
sciousness is a proof of his being alive.
We reply that it may be very good evidence to himself,
but it is not good evidence to us, nor would a rational
man attempt to use it in that way.

Our friend answers, "I work, and my work dem-
onstrates that I am." Precisely so, and God's works
demonstrate that *he* is. Quickly the reply comes, "But
you see me work, and you don't see God." To which
we answer: We by no means see *you* work; your body
is not yourself; your true self we have never seen. Your
mind executes its purposes through your external
frame, and we see your limbs moving, but the soul that
moves them is out of sight. It is a mystery of mysteries
how a spiritual subsistence, such as the mind, should
be able to operate upon matter.

The initial impression of mind upon matter is a
secret which no mortal has unveiled. You cannot prove

the existence of your soul to another man except by the same arguments that prove the being of God.

If then you stretch your wings for a flight of doubt, be brave enough to fly onward to the *ultima Thule* (distant unknown region; extreme limit). Doubt your own existence. Doubt whether you doubt; doubt whether there be any *you* to doubt; doubt whether there be anything to be doubted. A thorough-going agnostic shouldn't be sure that he is an agnostic; he should not in fact be too confident that he is himself or that he exists at all.

No Soul

A certain preacher had worked his best to benefit his audience, but one person came to him and somewhat rudely remarked, "Your preaching is of no use to me. I do not believe that I have a soul; I don't want to be talked to about an imaginary hereafter; I shall die like a dog."

The minister calmly replied, "Sir, I have evidently failed by misunderstanding. I did my best for the good of all my hearers, but I prepared the message under the notion that I was catering to men with souls. Had I known that there were creatures present who had no souls and would die like dogs, I would have provided a good supply of bones for them."

"Banter," says one. "Common sense," we say. What more gentle dealing than playful sarcasm can be expected by men who hold such degrading views of themselves? Assuredly no soul needs to be worried by them. They confess their own inability to help us and tacitly admit that we are not bound to let them hinder us.

"There is no such thing as light," cries one, "for I have no eyes with which to enjoy it." Is there any argument in this? No, the blind gentleman is to be pitied, but his opinions on color and optics can have no weight. Soulless beings may hold what philosophies they please; their opinions may be interesting as curiosities, but they cannot influence men with souls in the least degree.

God in the Sphere of Our Life

When we trust in God, we are not exercising a dreamy dependence upon a faraway and inactive power. It is asked whether God ever operates on behalf of those who trust him, and it is hinted that he is otherwise occupied – that he will not stoop to the petty cares of men and women. Obviously this is an error. God's work is at our doors and in our chambers – yes, in our bodies and in our minds. The child's father is very busy, but he is busy in the room where his child needs him; therefore, he is where he is wanted.

The ordinary talk is about the operations of nature. Pray, sir, what is nature? The gentleman who has used the term looks around with surprise. He stutters, and stammers, and says that everybody knows what nature is.

"Tell us, then, what it is."

"Why," says he, "it is easy enough. Nature is . . . nature is nature." The truth is that the real worker is God himself, and any other force than his own power is nowhere to be found. The movements around us are not produced by laws as simpletons say; laws do nothing. They are neither more nor less than certain observed occurrences of the great Creator's working. But he himself does the work. We may trust him to work *for* us who is working all *around* us. *I will praise thee; for I am fearfully and wonderfully made; marvellous are thy works, and that, my soul knows right well* (Psalm 139:14).

The Great God Answers Faith

Moreover, we may not refuse reliance upon God on the grounds of our insignificance, for it is not conceivable that anything is too little for God. The wonders of the microscope are quite as remarkable as those of the telescope: we may not set a boundary on the Lord in one direction any more than in the other. He can and will show his divine skill in a man's life as well as in a planet's orbit.

Witnesses are alive who testify to the Lord's making bare his arm on behalf of them that trust him. Any man may also put the principle to the test in his own instance, and it is remarkable that none have done so in vain. There are no reasons in his character why God should not answer to his creatures' confidence; there are many reasons why he should. At any rate, as far as we are concerned, we are ready to put it to the test and to let the experiment last throughout our whole existence. *In the day of my trouble I will call upon thee, for thou wilt answer me* (Psalm 86:7).

Why God Is Not Relied On

Doesn't it seem peculiar that so few men should lovingly

grasp the idea of linking their lives to God in faith? Why is this? The severe moralist would rightly answer that it is because they have no desire to lead lives that are connected to God; they don't seek purity, truth, justice, and holiness as God's energy would work in them. Doubtless, this is the case, but don't let it be true of us. Virtue is so admirable that we cannot have too much of it, and the fact that the divine power moves us towards goodness is one of its chief attractions in the eyes of reasonable men. *Finally, brethren, whatever things are true, whatever things are honest, whatever things are just, whatever things are pure, whatever things are lovely, whatever things are of good report, if there is any virtue and if there is any praise, exercise yourselves in these things* (Philippians 4:8).

We Shouldn't Be Despondent

There may be some who are not so averse to goodness as they are despondent or hopeless about attaining it. To these it may be helpful to remember that despondency is unwarranted when God is involved in a matter. In this case no doubt should enter, for God can raise the most polluted to innocence, because he is able to do all things.

> *He stretches out the north wind over the empty place and hangs the earth upon nothing. He binds up the waters in his thick clouds; and the cloud is not rent under them. He holds back the face of his throne and spreads his cloud upon it. He has compassed*

*the waters with bounds until the end of light
and darkness. The pillars of heaven tremble
and are astonished at his reproof. He divides
the sea with his power, and by his intelligence he smites its pride. By his spirit he has
adorned the heavens; his hand has formed
the fleeing serpent. Behold, these are parts
of his ways; but how little a portion have we
heard of him? For the thunder of his power,
who shall understand?* (Job 26:7-14)

It is appalling to refuse to rely upon God because we
do not wish to be pure; it is dishonoring to his glory to
decline confidence in his power to elevate us because
we are still so unrighteous. God is good, and a char-
acteristic of a good being is that
he desires to make others good.
God is omnipotent, and his power
governs the world of the mind as
well as that of matter. Both will and
ability are united in God concern-
ing the object of our desire – namely, the purity and
usefulness of our lives. Therefore, we may fly to him
with a cheerful readiness and rest in him with much
hopefulness.

> It is appalling to refuse to rely upon God because we do not wish to be pure.

Further Causes of Unbelief

Secretly, men have a confidence somewhere, even when
they refuse to rely upon God. They have made gods of
themselves and have come to rest in self-sufficiency. He
who has never seen his own face may easily believe in

its superior beauty, if he is aided therein by flatterers. So a man who doesn't know his own heart may readily form a high opinion of his own excellence and find confidence in his own wisdom – a plant of rapid growth. *Who changed the truth of God into a lie and worshipped and served the creature rather than the Creator, who is blessed for all ages* (Romans 1:25).

This is one of the worst enemies of faith. He who can always rely upon himself has no patience with talk about faith in God; he relegates that lowly stuff to underlings. He is of a more stately mold. His self-restraint is perfect; his judgment is infallible; his appreciation of the morally beautiful is fully developed. He is a self-made man and is both his own providence and rewarder.

"Tut – the man is a fool!" Quick and sensible minds speak thus impatiently; and the cooler observations of the charitable are sorrowfully driven to confirm their verdict. *Professing themselves to be wise, they became fools* (Romans 1:22). We, with whom the reader now communes, are not such grand, self-governing infallibles. We fear that our appetites and passions may betray us, that our reason may misguide us, that our prejudices may impede us, and that our surroundings may thwart us. Therefore, most deliberately would we look to the Strong for strength and cast our folly upon the wisdom of the Eternal. Of course, we shall not expect imitators among the vainglorious, the frivolous, and the fancifully perfect.

The Sneer

Sneers are poor, contemptible things; they are not born in good men's bosoms, and most wise men despise them when leveled at themselves. They break no bones, and men of backbone smile at them. Yet with the weaker sort, they are terrible weapons of war, and the dread of them has made more cowards than the roar of cannons.

When faith in God is sneered at, the exhibition is a wretched one, verging on the utmost degree of imbecility. To trust a quack is excused, but to trust the Almighty is reviled. People who never question their own wisdom laugh to scorn those who rest in the wisdom of the Lord. In such a case, it ought to be easy for a man with common sense to stand bravely. Laugh at a creature for believing his Creator? That is to despise the plainest argument of reason, to dispute an axiom, and to assail a truism – as well as ridicule a man for mathematical accuracy, honesty, and learning, or despise an engineer for trusting the laws of gravitation or a farmer for depending upon the return of the harvest. Of course, if men like to be slaves, they will pay attention to the jeers of the foolish; but we write for men who can say from their hearts:

> I had as lief not be as live to be
> In awe of such a thing as I myself.[5]

More Knowledge of God Desirable

However willing a man may be to put his trust in God,

---

5   William Shakespeare, *Julius Caesar*.

his faith must largely depend upon his knowledge. *So then faith comes by hearing, and the ear to hear by the word of God* (Romans 10:17). It is almost impossible to have confidence in a Great Unknown. The variety and breadth of our knowledge of God will help faith in exercising herself upon matters that a narrow knowledge would exclude from the list of practical objects. What we perceive in creation might well cause us to rely upon God's power, if we could be sure that it would be exerted on our behalf. But what if there is a doubt on that point? What we observe in Providence may reasonably cause us to depend upon the divine goodness, unless we have rendered it necessary for that goodness to withhold itself. A conscientious man may not consider this improbable. If our knowledge of God is confined to his greatness, goodness, and wisdom, we are already in an awkward condition, for we have not yet met with that divine quality that can satisfy a certain uneasiness of which we are painfully conscious. As our heart suspects that we are not all that we ought to be, we need to know far more of God if we are to enjoy a comfortable confidence in him.

How Is More to Be Known?

All probability goes to show that the more we know of God, the easier it will be for us to put our trust in him. The quality of goodness so exceeds in the known that we expect the same to pervade the unknown. But how is more knowledge to be obtained?

Can we go from nature up to nature's God? Perhaps.

But it would be a far more effectual business if nature's God would come down to us and be his own expositor. No man can be altogether known by his works, much less can God. God's universe is so immense that if it could be proved to be a full revealing of himself, it would be too vast for our mental grasp. How can we know all that the universe would teach?

The works of God are too many for us to know them all. How then can we learn the many-sided wisdom that they would reveal? If they were replicas, we might learn all from one; but as they are infinitely various, our capacity is overflooded, and there is urgent need that divine superiority should make an abstract for us and communicate it in a manner suited to our nature.

God Revealing Himself

If it is a natural thing for the intelligent creature to trust in his Creator, and if it is necessary for that trust that he gain more knowledge of the Creator than he can gather by observing his works, isn't it reasonable to suppose that the wise and beneficent Creator will enable his intelligent creatures to know him? At least so far as may be required for the purposes of faith? As Paul prayed, *that the God of our Lord Jesus Christ, the Father of glory, may give unto you the spirit of wisdom and revelation in the knowledge of him; illuminating the eyes of your understanding, that*

> God's universe is so immense that if it could be proved to be a full revealing of himself, it would be too vast for our mental grasp.

ye may know what is the hope of his calling and what are the riches of the glory of his inheritance in the saints and what is the exceeding greatness of his power in us who believe, by the operation of the power of his strength (Ephesians 1:17-19).

If it were essential to the well-being of his subjects that a king should be personally known to them, we cannot conceive of a good monarch shutting himself up entirely from public view or refusing to address his people. True, the glory of God does not need man's observation; nor may we suppose that God's motive could be selfish in seeking to be known. But since man's feeble condition needs a divine revelation, it is not unreasonable to hope that One who is supremely good would make himself known. The manifestation of God in his works of providence by giving stability, fruitfulness, or food is abundantly sufficient and more than sufficient for rocks and trees and animals. But for intelligent minds there must be a manifestation of God to the soul and spirit, or faith under many forms would be impossible, and the soul would be left in a forlorn condition. Such a forsaking of the work of his own hands we do not expect from the infinitely good God.

Revelation in Words

Language is the best means of communication between one mind and another. It is, therefore, natural that God should use the best means of communication and converse with men in words. *Thy word is a lamp unto my feet and a light unto my way* (Psalm 119:105). Language that is reduced to writing becomes more accurate and more permanent; hence, it is in every sense most probable that when the infinite God communicates with finite men, it should be in the speech of men, and this speech should be preserved in writing. Divine writings do not, therefore, come to us apart from the expected order of God's procedure; the announcement of their existence does not create any overwhelming surprise, nor do we see in the notion of such writings anything forced and abnormal.

A mind entirely locked up in itself could hardly belong to an energetic worker. He who makes, is pretty sure to communicate, and it seems right to expect that so generous a Maker as the Most High God would also converse with other minds, even though they might be inferior and subordinate, especially upon a topic so needful as his own nature and requirements. *The exposition of thy words gives light; it gives understanding unto the simple* (Psalm 119:130). One does not expect to hear of a great artist that he is a hermit; the qualities of a great worker are such that produce a friend, a brother, or a father. We may expect the Creator to be communicative. True, a clever workman may never speak, for he may happen to be deaf and dumb; but he that made all ears and tongues is not such a case.

The Book Should Be Examined

If there were nothing more than a rumor floating about respectable society that a book had been inspired by God as a revelation of his own character, thoughts, and will, an honest man, desirous to be right in his life, would speedily and with great care examine the claims of the much-needed writing. *O how I love thy law! it is my meditation all the day.* (Psalm 119:97). The Book venerated by our fathers, which claims to be the Word of God, has been accepted as such by so vast a number of wise and righteous men that we cannot speak of its appearance as a mere matter of rumor. *All scripture is given by inspiration of God and is profitable for doctrine, for reproof, for correction, for instruction in righteousness, that the man of God may be perfect, thoroughly furnished unto all good works* (2 Timothy 3:16-17). It has been long before the world, and it has been reverently received by many of the best of our race.

Effects of the Book

The effect that this Book has produced in the nations that have given it even a partial obedience is very remarkable. They are far advanced in comparison to those who give it a secondary place, and they are out of sight ahead of those who are not acquainted with it. The result that follows its introduction in our own day to the most savage people is beyond all question exceedingly beneficial. Nobody can doubt that the South Sea Islands have been lifted out of the worst savagery by the teaching of this volume.

We have not yet heard of any other book producing such effects, and thus the volume is pressed upon our attention by the undeniable results of its influence, both in former ages and in our own times. It is very easy to discover people whose entire character has been changed by reading this Book and easier still to find individuals who assert that it is their comfort under all circumstances, their guide out of all difficulties, and the priceless food of their spirits.

Many other books have been warmly praised by their readers, but we have never yet met with any other volume which has commanded such frequent enthusiasm and such devoted affection as the Bible. Neither have we heard of one which answers so many and such diverse purposes in connection with the lives of men.

Seeing for One's Self

We are not too severe when we demand that each man should read the Bible for himself. *Study to show thyself approved unto God, a workman that has nothing to be ashamed of, rightly dividing the word of truth* (2 Timothy 2:15). In testing a book that professes to be the revelation of God's mind, we'd be acting unworthily if we trusted this to others – whoever they may be. Secondhand information lacks assurance and vividness; a personal investigation is far more satisfactory and beneficial. The highly superior person who dismisses the whole matter with a final verdict that closes the argument before it is opened is probably not as cultured a being as he professes to be. At any rate, he lacks the judicial mind so helpful in the pursuit of truth. Does

> We are not too severe when we demand that each man should read the Bible for himself.

our wisdom decide a matter before it hears it? *For him that answers a word before he hears, it is folly and reproach unto him* (Proverbs 18:13).

Nature demands attention, hard and persevering, from those who desire to be true scientists; the Word of God certainly deserves as reverent an investigation as his works. Why shouldn't the Scriptures be studied thoroughly? Even as mere literature they will reward the scholar's care. It is typical of a wise man to calmly and earnestly search those famous writings that are cherished by so many masterminds. The voice that cried to Augustine, "*Tolle lege!*" (Take up and read) was no sound of folly. To take up and read a great and good book cannot be to our detriment.

Reading That the Book Deserves

It would be disgraceful to borrow secondhand criticisms and turn the Bible away unheard. It shouldn't be read hurriedly, for that is not fair to any author who is dealing seriously with weighty subjects. A book which masterminds have reverenced can only be despised by fools.

> *My son, if thou wilt receive my words and hide my commandments within thee so that thou incline thine ear unto wisdom and apply thine heart to intelligence, yea, if thou criest for understanding and givest thy voice unto intelligence, if thou seekest her as silver and searchest for her as for hid treasures, then shalt thou understand the fear of the LORD*

and find the knowledge of God. For the LORD gives wisdom; out of his mouth comes knowledge and intelligence. (Proverbs 2:1-6)

To read the Book is to feel that it is full of power; a man would have to be willfully wicked to refuse this verdict, even if he hated that power.

This Book has more thought in it than its opponents could have displayed. Their counter-thought is only Bible truth turned upside down, and therefore it owes its origin to the Book it assails.

A singular fact may be mentioned: It is certain that those who love this Book best are those who have read it most. As a general rule, those who rail against it have not acquired more than a scanty knowledge of it.

More Than Reading Needed

Much of the instruction contained in the material universe can be discerned by the eye of the thoughtful observer, but a portion of its secrets no man can ascertain, because for the discovery of much scientific truth, experiment is needed. The chemist, for instance, will acquire little knowledge if he does not engage in tests and analyses. We will not, therefore, restrict ourselves to mere reading in the pursuit of truth. The Lord told Joshua that *This book of the law shall not depart out of thy mouth, but thou shalt meditate therein day and night that thou may keep and do according to all that is written therein; for then thou shalt make thy way to prosper, and then thou shalt understand everything* (Joshua 1:8).

If the Scriptures ask for experiment or experience, we shall be prepared to perform or to undergo the required processes if possible. Christian teachers everywhere tell us that the religion of the Bible cannot be known except by experience, and that statement is not different from when the chemist sends us to the laboratory and the crucible. To be able to trust God we must know him; to obtain that knowledge we desire a revelation. Given the revelation, it requires us to let it renew our mind. Shall we draw back? No. If there is a truth to be known, we wish to know it; if there is a life to be received, we would receive it; if there is a perfect way to be found, we would follow it.

Style of the Bible

He who begins to read the Bible at the Gospel of John would be met by such words as *In the beginning was the Word, and the Word was with the God, and the Word was God* (John 1:1). If he is candid in spirit and cultured in mind, he would be struck with the sublime simplicity of the language and the fathomless depth of the meaning. There is a case on record of an instantaneous conversion to faith in God by the first hearing of these wondrous words. We need not wonder why.

It little matters where the reading begins; let the volume fall open as if by chance, and the reader will still discover the same singular majesty of style. It is unique. Although the many books that compose the library called the Bible were written by some forty or more authors, and each writer had his own idiosyncrasy of utterance, yet the style of the entire volume is one. It is indeed singular that the unity of tone should be so eminently preserved amid the plurality of voices.

We venture to say the Bible style is singularly independent and altogether inimitable. It would be impossible for any man to compose a supplement to the Pentateuch, dictate another gospel, or even write another epistle. The fabrication has been tried, but there has been no chance of palming it off upon readers of the Scriptures. Forgeries of great authors have been common, and some of them have nearly succeeded. The church has disposed of all attempts to force apocryphal books upon her with far less difficulty than the literary world has been able to dispose of forgeries of Shakespeare.

> We venture to say the Bible style is singularly independent and altogether inimitable.

Neither the honesty nor the religiousness of men would have prevented the crime of adding vile inventions to the sacred books of the Old and New Testaments. The attempt itself must forever be ineffective because of the impossibility of an impostor's imitating that style of perfect truth that is peculiar to the Word of God. We cannot imagine a mere man speaking after the manner of God; for certain, no uninspired person has yet spoken in the style of the Holy Spirit.

We can trust an ordinary schoolboy to detect the wide difference between any apocryphal or pretended sacred book and the writings of an inspired psalmist, prophet, or apostle. The notion that the Vedas of the

Brahmins, the Avesta of Zoroaster, and the Koran of Muhammad are comparable in style or manner to the Word of God is ridiculous. Max Müller tells us that those who believe "that these are books full of primeval wisdom and religious enthusiasm, or at least of sound and simple moral teaching, will be disappointed on consulting these volumes." Neither can the uncouth rhyme of a clown be mistaken for the stately verse of Milton, or the noblest language of man be thought by an instructed mind to be the utterance of God.

The style of Scripture is never stilted nor bombastic, yet it has a quiet, unpretentious royalty all its own; this sets the Bible altogether apart from other works and marks it as the king of books. Far from being fettered by conventionalities, it is as free as the air, and yet its music is ever tuned to the same harmonies. It is varied – joyous, accusatory, plaintive, descriptive, simple, and intricate; yet it remains in every phase true to its own style – ever human but at the same moment always divine.

Fullness of the Book

One of the marvels of the Bible is its singular fullness. It is not a book of gold leaf beaten thin, as most books are in regard to thought, but its sentences are nuggets of unalloyed truth. The Book of God is clearly the god of books, for it is infinite. A German author once said, "In this little book is contained all the wisdom of the world."

We search the world for truth; we cull
> The good, the pure, the beautiful,
From graven stone and written scroll,
> From all old flower-fields of the soul;
And, weary seekers of the best,
> We come back laden from the quest,
To find that all the sages said
> Is in the Book our mothers read.[6]

Two intellectuals held a brief discussion as to which of all books they would prefer in prison if they were shut up and only had the choice of one and could not obtain another for twelve months. The first made a sensible selection when he proposed to take Shakespeare as his companion, for that great author's works are brimming with fresh thought and masterly expression. But we think the second man gave an unanswerable reason for preferring the Bible. "Why," said his friend, "you do not believe in it!"

"No," said he, "but whether I believe in it or not, it is no end of a book."

We thank him for that word; it is indeed "no end of a book." Its range of subjects is boundless, and its variety of treatment is indescribable. Its depth of thought and height of expression are immeasurable. It is altogether inexhaustible. It is a million times magnified Bodleian of teaching, and its *Bibline,* or biblical content, is of the most concentrated kind.[7] The Scripture has inci-

---

6   John Greenleaf Whittier, "The Book Our Mothers Read."
7   Bodleian is the library of Oxford University, reestablished by Thomas Bodley, an English diplomat and scholar, 1545-1613.

dentally suggested masses of human literature, and it is the actual material of books to an extent that few would credit. It contains vast stores of what we may call *mother of thought.*

After being catechized, criticized, caricatured, and crucified for all these centuries, it still remains a new book, beginning its circulation rather than ending it. Jesus proclaimed, *Heaven and earth shall pass away, but my words shall not pass away* (Mark 13:31). When the world grows older and wiser and attains to the sixth form of its school, the sacred volume will be its final classic, just as it was its first handbook when the newborn Hebrew nation spelled out the rudiments of truth and righteousness.

Test the Bible

Let the Book be tried by its internal evidences, and let its undesigned coincidences be thoroughly studied. Their richness is deeply interesting; some readers prefer the observation of those to the reading of the last new novel.

Let the Book be tried by ancient records and memorials. Is it correct in historical matters where it would have surely failed had it been of human concoction? Providence has arranged for its frequent testing by historical records. In Egypt, Palestine, Moab, Bashan, and Nineveh, fresh inscriptions and monumental sculptures are being found, and as these are brought to the surface, they cry out as witnesses for scriptural history. With what delight would a slab have been welcomed from any mound or catacomb that would have contradicted Moses or the prophets, but as yet the sacred record has been vindicated. *For all flesh is as grass, and all the glory of man as the flower of grass. The grass withers, and its flower falls away, but the word of the Lord endures for ever. And this is the word which by the gospel is preached unto you* (1 Peter 1:24-25).

More recently, certain bitter biblical opponents have strung together a number of Scripture's supposed blunders. The work has been carried out with acrid hate and with magnifying glasses of a high power, but the result is nil. Reading with fairness, the mind is annoyed by the recklessness of the objections, the arrogance of the objector, and the ignorance that is imputed to the audience. It would be easy to refute the charges laid against the historical accuracy of Scripture, but it can be an endless work when men do not desire to know the actual facts.

Influence As an Excellent Test

The better test is that which believers alone are able to describe. How has the Scripture influenced them? Has it flattered their conceit, lowered their ideal of virtue, nourished their selfishness, or discouraged their hopes of better things? No. They find God as revealed in the Book to be their Father and their Friend, and his methods of righteousness to be most elevating and purifying. They are enabled to trust him in their struggles for that which is good and noble and always find their faith abundantly justified. Day by day, they see for themselves that God's declarations are true and that they are accompanied with power.

The words of God awaken echoes in our hearts. The Book is omniscient and omnipresent, like the Spirit that inspired it; it knows all about us and tells us our secret thoughts. It must be divine, for it touches secret springs known only to him who fashioned the heart in the beginning. He who knows the Book has watched the fouling of its machinery so closely that its present movements cannot deceive him, and he speaks as only such an observer

> The words of God awaken echoes in our hearts.

could do. The Bible revelation meets our needs and allays our fears – not the shallow wants and dreads of worldly frivolity but the deep and terrible necessities of a mind ready to despair through a crushing sense of past failure. This Book is a salvation for men doing business on great waters where trifles are out of the question. It is a guiding star to minds encompassed with the midnight of despair. O matchless revelation of truth, if you did not come from God, where did you come from? If all you tell us is a dream, gladly would we dream again or die in our sleep! Until now we have found all your teaching true to our inner life, and we cannot but bear witness to the fact! *The beginning of thy word is truth, and every one of the judgments of thy righteousness is eternal* (Psalm 119:160).

The Sinless One

A clear proof of the divine origin of Scripture is in its

portrait of the perfect Man. Jesus is sinless in thought, and word, and deed; his enemies are unable to find a fault in him, either of excess or defect. Nowhere else in the world have we such another portrait of a man; it would be superfluous to say that nowhere have we such another man. Jesus is unique; he is original with peculiarities all his own but without any divergence from the straight line of integrity. He is not a recluse, whose character would have few relationships and therefore few tests, but he is one living in the fierce light of a King among men, coming into a relationship with the world in a thousand ways. He is a great ethical teacher, inculcating a system far surpassing any other and embodying it in his own life.

Above all, he is the crowning edifice of a perfect life with the surrender of himself to death for his enemies. *For he has made him to be sin for us, who knew no sin, that we might be made the righteousness of God in him* (2 Corinthians 5:21). Where did this portrait come from if the man never existed? No painter goes beyond his own ideal; no imperfect mind could have invented the perfect mind of Christ. The record is divine.

Science and the Book As One

Between the revelation of God in his Word and that in his works, there can be no actual discrepancy. The one may go further than the other, but the revelation must be harmonious. Between the interpretation of the works and the interpretation of the Word, there may be great differences. It must be admitted that men of the Book have sometimes missed its meaning; we have never held the doctrine of the infallibility of such men who are called scripturists. No, it is certain that in their desire to defend their Bible, devout persons have been unwise enough to twist its words or set them in an unnatural light in order to make the Book agree with the teachings of scientific men.

Herein lies their weakness. If they had always labored to understand what God said in his Book and had steadfastly adhered to its meaning, whatever might be advanced by the scientific, they would have been wise; and as professed science advanced towards real science, the fact that the old Book is right would have become more and more apparent. *O Timothy, keep that which is committed to thy trust, turn away from profane voices and vain things and arguments in the vain name of science, which some professing have erred concerning the faith* (1 Timothy 6:20-21).

Scientific Statements Not Infallible

Those who have addicted themselves to the study of nature and have despised the Word certainly cannot claim such immunity from mistake as to demand a revision of Scripture interpretation every time they adopt a new hypothesis. The history of philosophy, from the beginning until now, reads like a *Comedy of Errors*.[8] Each generation of learned men has been eminently successful in refuting all its predecessors, and there is every probability that much of what is

---

8   *The Comedy of Errors* is William Shakespeare's shortest play, which incorporates absurd humor.

now endorsed as orthodox scientific doctrine will be entirely upset in a few years' time. *For the wisdom of this world is foolishness with God. For it is written, He takes the wise in their own craftiness. And again, The Lord knows the thoughts of the wise, that they are vain* (1 Corinthians 3:19-20).

When we remember that one association of savants, or geniuses, has proved that there is no such thing as mind, and that another has been equally successful in proving that there is no such thing as matter, we are led to ask the question, "When doctors differ, who is to decide?"

Little Is Settled in Science

There are many voices in the world, some powerful and others weak, but there is not yet a consensus of thoughtful observers sufficiently strong to demonstrate any one system of science to be absolutely true. The inductive process of Bacon no doubt yields the nearest approach to certainty, but even this cannot raise a deduction beyond question, for no man of science knows all the instances that can be adduced.[9] His deduction from what he knows may be upset by equally sure inferences from what he does not know.

The time over which scientific observations can travel, even if it is extended into ages, is only as a watch in the night compared with the eternity of God. The range of human observation is but a drop in the bucket

---

9   Sir Francis Bacon (1561-1626) is credited with establishing the scientific method whereby a set of facts or observations of nature are used to determine laws of nature.

compared with the circle of the heavens. Therefore, it may turn out, in a thousand instances, that there are more things in heaven and earth than were ever dreamed of in the most accurate philosophy of scientists. From Aristotle on down, these good people have done their best, but they have hardly accomplished more than to prove us all dunces and themselves scarcely a fig better than the rest of us.

The range of human observation is but a drop in the bucket compared with the circle of the heavens.

Where Alteration Is Easiest

Instead of altering the Bible or allowing that it may be mistaken upon mundane matters, a far safer course is to continue the former process of amending science, which is made of a substance so flexible that no great effort is required to change its fashion to the reverse of its present shape. *For ever, O LORD, thy word is settled in the heavens. Thy truth is from generation to generation; thou hast established the earth, and it perseveres* (Psalm 119:89-90).

From the first doctor in the school of science down to the last, error has not only been possible but also almost unavoidable from the limitation of human faculties and the mystery of phenomena. Even the interpreters of Scripture have been less absurd than the interpreters of nature, though certain of these have gone to grievous lengths. Yet the Book retains its impregnable position. If it ever comes to a matter of decision whether we shall believe God's revelation or man's science, we shall unhesitatingly cry, *for God is true, and every man a liar* (Romans 3:4)!

No Remarkable Difficulty

At the present moment, we see no considerable difficulty. Scripture may not square with proposed hypotheses, but it agrees with known facts. Interpreted in an intelligent manner, Scripture displays as clear an agreement with nature and Providence as words can show with works. An article in the *Illustrated London News* may describe in words a scene which is depicted by the pencil of an accurate artist on the opposite page. The two forms of instruction may be completely consistent, and yet the impression upon the reader who fails to see the illustration may not be the same as that produced upon an observer who only notices the sketch and neglects the written word. The man who cared only for the typography might quarrel with the enthusiast of the woodblock, while the picture-observer might equally retort upon the reader. But if the two could be combined, the intent of the author would more surely be understood. Let him that reads the Word consider the work, and let him that observes nature attend to revelation, and growing wisdom shall be the reward of both.

Anchorage and Roothold of Faith

When the Bible is fully accepted as God's own revelation of himself, the mind has come to a quiet anchorage, and this is no small gain. A safe resting place is an urgent need of the soul. To find a sure foothold somewhere, men have tried to rest in an infallible church or in their own supposed infallible reason. Of two earnest brothers, one became a papist and another an infidel. We do not feel attracted to either haven, if either of these can be called a haven. We prefer for our own part to cast anchor once for all in an infallible revelation. Drifting about is injurious to character and fatal to influence; a roothold is essential, and here then is ours.

When first the anchor goes down, or the root strikes, little can be known of the anchorage or the soil, compared with that which will be discovered by the test of experience. Thousands are quietly moored in the Fair Havens of Scripture; myriads are growing and bearing fruit in the garden of the Lord. Their witness is assuring, but our own experience will bring the most satisfactory conviction.

Down goes the anchor; the rootlets embrace the soil.

Sin Disturbs Faith

Accepting Holy Scripture as God's revelation of himself, we now know more of him for practical purposes than we could have otherwise known and especially upon one matter not yet mentioned. Our conscience (for which we are most grateful, for our upward struggle would be hopeless without it) reminds us that we are not quite beginning life, for we have already proceeded some distance, though maybe not as we might desire to have done. With a sigh, our memory holds up various records, which we cannot look upon with dignity, but *forgetting those things which are behind and extending myself unto those things which are ahead, I press toward the mark for the prize of the high calling of God in Christ Jesus* (Philippians 3:13-14).

We may not have been the worst of men, but we are sorry that there should be any worse than we are. We have possibly steered clear of the rocks of vice, but into the whirlpool of indifference we have been drawn. We have not done our best, and we suspect that our best might not have been so very good if we had done it. Happily, this divinely inspired Book addresses the subject of sin and the effectual method by which the guilty can be purged of their defilement and equipped for clean walking in the future.

Here then we shall learn how the imperfect may dare to rely upon the Perfect and how the offender may venture to trust in him whom he has offended. Happy is the man who has been born to such knowledge and to the possibilities which are already discerned within it.

Prayer Suggested

When a new discovery of danger or advantage bursts upon a devout man, he is led to address God in some way. He prays or he praises, as the case may be, and this comes of very proper and natural instincts, especially when they are intelligently based upon the faith which is found within the soul. When we see that God has increased our knowledge by revealing himself through a book, and when we hear that he has cleared up a dark and difficult point that might have hindered faith, it is fitting for us to praise him.

This done, we should set about reading that priceless writing of his with earnest prayer for help in our understanding that we may perceive its meaning and for strength in our will that we may obey its precepts.

The Book is for our use, not for our amusement. It behooves us to handle such a gift after a worthy manner. It is not to be played with but to be put to most earnest, immediate, and continued use. It professes to guide us in this life as well as instruct us in the next. It must not therefore be laid aside as a pillow for some future day of death, but we must ask God to make it our present instrument for righteous living, our daily tutor in the art of shunning evil and attaining good. *With what shall a young man cleanse his way? when he shall keep thy word* (Psalm 119:9).

The Book is for our use, not for our amusement.

Removal of the Great Obstacle to Faith

Concerning the consciousness of evil in our past and the tendency to wrongdoing in our nature, the Bible is very clear; it is most explicit as to God's way of removing this hindrance to our future progress. In Holy Scripture we see a wise and gracious method for the putting away of guilt without injury to the divine justice. The atonement offered by the Lord Jesus, who is the essence of the revelation of God, is an eminently satisfactory solution to the soul's sternest problem. Our feeling is that God, the universal Ruler, must do right and must not, even for mercy's sake, relax the rule that says evil works will bring evil as its consequence. When in our best frame of mind, we would not wish to have this beneficial law abolished for our own sake. Sin ought to be punished; let the rule stand, come what may. *For the wages of sin is death, but the grace of God is eternal life in Christ Jesus our Lord* (Romans 6:23). An unrighteous God would be the most terrible of conceivable evils. Sin linked with reward or divorced from ill consequences would be the death of the great principle of righteousness, which is the aspiration of all perfect moral sanity.

Scripture proposes no abolition of law or relaxation of penalty, but it reveals the plan of substitution. The offended Judge bears in his own person the consequences of the offense of rebel man. He assumes human nature, that in his own person human sin may receive chastisement. He bears the burden of human transgression, and concerning him we read these divine words: *the chastisement of our peace was upon him; and by his stripes healing was provided for us* (Isaiah 53:5). The whole transaction of substitution, descending to death upon the shameful tree and rising into resurrection and ascension, is a great marvel. It cannot be a fiction, for it surpasses all invention; it is the fact of facts. Carefully studied, looked at, and weighed, the sacrifice of himself by the Son of God carries into many minds a conviction not to be resisted and works a peace only to be conceived by those who enjoy it. Accepting the sacrifice that God has accepted, we ourselves are accepted of the Lord. *For he has made him to be sin for us, who knew no sin, that we might be made the righteousness of God in him* (2 Corinthians 5:21).

God's Method of Mercy

Forgiveness of sin through an atonement satisfies a dim but true decision of humanity in favor of justice – a decision which is nearly unanimous in all races. Even the unenlightened consciences of savage heathen yearn that wrongs committed are swiftly avenged. As a rule, man does not dare to approach God without a sacrifice. The more enlightened mind is not content without a measure of explanation as to the need and result of sacrifice; such explanation is given with great emphasis in the inspired Scripture.

The vicarious death of the Son of God, when understood and accepted, yields such peace to the believer that he feels as much at ease as if the law had never been broken. *Christ has redeemed us from the curse of the law, being made a curse for us* (Galatians 3:13). By the death of the divine victim, the law is so vindicated that it stands higher in the veneration of the universe than if its full punishment had been exacted.

The heart is therefore quieted once for all upon sound principles to which conscience gives its full assent. Jesus has put away sin by an atonement that is the marvel of eternity, and there is no more cause for dread to the believer than Samson had reason to be afraid when the dead lion lay at his feet full of honey.

Faith's Earliest Work

As guilt is removed by faith in God when he is revealed in Christ Jesus, the mind is overwhelmed with gratitude for the great love displayed in the gift of the great propitiation, and it is moved to an intense hate of the evil which required such a sacrifice. But, *In this does the charity consist, not because we had loved God, but because he loved us and has sent his Son to be the reconciliation for our sins* (1 John 4:10). This immediately initiates a purging or cleansing, the like of which the heart has never known. In the blaze of divine goodness, the pleasure once felt in sin is dried up and utterly evaporated.

Out of the midst of that consuming fire, there leaps forth a newborn passion for righteousness, born of the immortal flame of infinite love. This becomes a motivating force for a higher life, surprising to the receiver who is amazed at the joy and the hope which abound within him. The stronger the faith in the revealed propitiation, the fuller the rest and the more intense the energetic desire for perfect holiness. To trust God is now an instinct, and to rely upon the Lord Jesus Christ becomes a joy, as we read his cheering words, *ye believe in God, believe also in me* (John 14:1).

Faith Delights in a Plain Gospel

It is a matter for deep gratitude that the gospel is as plain as a pikestaff[10]. If it had been intended to be a secret remedy for an elite few, it would have been obscure

---

10   Meaning, "very obvious."

and philosophical. But it is meant for the poor, the illiterate, and the undeveloped, and therefore it must be what it is – simplicity itself. *The exposition of thy words gives light; it gives understanding unto the simple* (Psalm 119:130). Thank God, the gospel does not lend itself to quackery!

To hear our fashionable thinkers talk, one might suppose the gospel to be an exclusive and aristocratic system for their excellencies to amuse themselves with whenever they might choose to develop it a little further. We are glad to find the gospel in the Scriptures in the form of a plain, common sense, perfect doctrine that has saved millions already, is saving multitudes at the present moment, and will save myriads when all its superfine critics are disintegrating in their graves.

Sometimes faith has great need of patience when it is pestered with objections against a system that is in grand operation and proves itself by its results. Why don't these objectors raise an outcry against the sun? Why not deny that it gives either light or heat?

Faith's Discovery

When the newborn faith has wondered for a while, she asks herself the question, "Where did I come from? How did I come into the heart?" The answer that she receives from the Book and from her own consciousness is *of the operation of God* (Colossians 2:12). The Holy Spirit must have worked this faith, which is so new, so vivid, so potent, and so much above the ordinary range of the mind. If this is so, a new source of reliance is opened up. The man says, "God has actually begun to operate upon my nature, and as he is unchangeable, he will carry on this work and complete it."

Thereupon reliance on God enters a fertile country, a land which flows with milk and honey. The holy alliance is an actual fact. The Father must have drawn, or the man would not have come to Christ; and herein is love. The Christ has made a complete atonement for sin; and herein is love. The Holy Spirit has worked faith and its blessed consequences; and herein is love. The believing heart is introduced into a new relationship to God; it has reached an unexpected nearness to him; it has received the firstfruits of the power which it desired to rely upon. That same Spirit, who is in the heart, is declared to be an abiding Comforter, a Sanctifier, an inward and effectual Teacher. This makes the future quite different from what it had ever threatened or even promised to be. The revelation of the Book has become a revelation within the heart. The man believes after a higher fashion and is provided with a strength that his most sanguine hopes had never dreamed of realizing.

> The revelation of the Book has become a revelation within the heart.

Radical Change of Faith

Trusting in the Lord Jesus Christ for complete salvation and being assured that he is thereby saved, the believer comes under a new master principle. *If anyone is in Christ, they are a new creation: old things are passed away;*

behold, all things are made new (2 Corinthians 5:17). Before he knew he was redeemed by Christ, he labored for his own salvation; his every budding virtue had self for its goal. He acted or abstained from action, was just or generous, and praised God or prayed to him with the one design of benefiting himself. How little real virtue could be found in deeds proceeding from such a motive!

Yet from that motive, the worker could not be set free with any safety, unless by saving him the Lord could lift him beyond the need of seeking self-salvation and then cause him to pursue things noble and benevolent from pure love of God and man. It is natural that while a man is in danger, he should look mainly to his own safety; hence, nature itself is at first the enemy of unselfish virtue. But when the man's best interests are graciously secured, and he is set above all hazards, he looks beyond himself to his Deliverer and regulates his life not by selfishness but by gratitude. He sees himself as Paul did when he said, *I am crucified with Christ; nevertheless I live; yet not I, but Christ lives in me, and the life which I now live in the flesh I live by the faith of the Son of God, who loved me and gave himself for me* (Galatians 2:20). This is a grand uplifting of our manhood from oppressive fear to filial love. No mere animalism will ever understand a passion like that of St. Francis Xavier:

> My God, I love thee; not because
> I hope for heaven thereby,

Nor because those who love thee not
    Must burn eternally.

Thou, O my Jesus, thou didst me
    Upon the cross embrace;
For me didst bear the nails and spear,
    And manifold disgrace,

And griefs and torments numberless,
    And sweat of agony;
Yea, death itself, and all for one
    Who was thine enemy.

Then why, O Blessed Jesus Christ,
    Should I not love thee well?
Not for the hope of winning heaven,
    Nor of escaping hell.

In grateful love we have a fulcrum for the moral lever, a principle noble and elevating, strong enough to produce works of infinitely more value than any that can come from the slavish dread of punishment or the mercenary hope of reward.

Faith and the Nature of Christ

No concept of the Lord Jesus Christ approaches correctness without seeing in his one person the two natures of God and man united. A practical faith has its most ample help in that person in whom the Godhead and the Manhood were blended but not confused. Jesus sympathizes with the condition in which the straggler who pursues excellence finds himself, for he also *was in all points tempted like as we are, yet without sin* (Hebrews 4:15). Jesus knows the difficulties that grow out of the infirmities of flesh and blood, for he felt sickness and pain, poverty and hunger, weakness and depression. And, *No temptation has taken you but such as is common to man, but God is faithful, who will not suffer you to be tempted above what ye are able but will with the temptation also make a way to escape, that ye may be able to bear it* (1 Corinthians 10:13). It is a great gain in a human career, a specially suitable assistance, to have an unlimited power at one's side sympathizing with our weakness.

The advantage is not less in the other direction, for here is a Man who is bound to us by the most intense relationship and affection. He is not only tender to the last degree of our suffering nature but is also as wise as he is brotherly; he is as mighty to subdue our faults as he is gentle to bear with our frailties. His Manhood brings Jesus down to us, but united with the divine nature it lifts us up to God. The Lord Jesus thus not only ministers to our comfort but also to our betterment, which is the greater concern of the two.

Could faith believe in a being more answerable to all our needs, more helpful to our noblest longings? Allied to Jesus, we confidently aspire to such likeness to our Creator as it is possible for a creature to bear.

Enthusiasm for the Person of Jesus

The love of the believer for the Lord Jesus is intensely personal and enthusiastic. It rises above all other affections. His love, his sufferings, his perfections, and his glories fill the heart and set it on fire. There is more force in the love of an actual living person than in acceptance of any set of doctrines however important they may be. The courage of a leader has often produced daring deeds which no philosophy could have demanded. Our glorious leader, Christ Jesus, inspires his followers with a burning passion, an all-consuming zeal, and an irrepressible enthusiasm which supplies all the energy that the noblest life can need. It is no small aid to our noblest ambition to have our hearts captured by incarnate holiness.

> It is no small aid to our noblest ambition to have our hearts captured by incarnate holiness.

Faith in the Life of Christ on Earth

The more we examine the character of the Lord Jesus Christ, the more we are filled with admiration of it. In the Gospels is a fourfold photograph of his countenance, taken from different positions. Putting these together, or even meditating upon any one of them, we are charmed with its singular beauty. This is not at all remarkable, for almost every man in the world – believer or unbeliever – has acknowledged the singular excellence of the life of Christ. It is so original, so transcendent, and so perfect that all men, except certain blinded partisans sworn to run amok at all things holy, have bowed before its glory and regarded it as the model of excellence of perfect manhood.

In Scripture this is set before us as an example; therefore, it is imitable or worthy of being imitated. Better still, it is set forth as the ordained pattern to which the believer is to be conformed as God's great work is done. As Paul said, *Be ye followers of me, even as I also am of Christ* (1 Corinthians 11:1). To have a high ideal, to be assured that we can reach it, and to have a capable Helper who will enable us to reach that ideal is to have a grand assistance towards a life of virtue. Faith in this Exemplar, who is also our Savior, must administer strength in our life battle. To aspire to such a perfect character as the salvation which we most desire, is to be already saved in principle. It is a great comfort to be fired with an ambition to be like Jesus. Every selfish wretch may wish for salvation from hell to heaven; but to be saved from selfishness into the image of Christ is that which only the renewed in heart are pining for, and by that pining their salvation is assured.

Faith in the Principles of Christ's Life

It is observable that the self-denial of our Lord Jesus, which was complete and entire beyond all suspicion, proved to be for him the way to that preeminence of glory which he now enjoys.

> *Let this mind be in you, which was also in*
> *Christ Jesus, who, being in the form of God,*
> *thought it not robbery to be equal with God,*

*but emptied himself, taking the form of a
slave, made in the likeness of men, and being
found in fashion as a man, he humbled himself and became obedient unto death, even
the death of the cross.* (Philippians 2:5-8)

He is above all things because he stooped to the low-
est and meanest state. It is his honor that he laid aside
his glory and bowed to the greatest shame and scorn.
His glory in the hearts of his redeemed is that he made
himself of no reputation, took upon himself the form
of a servant, and even died – the Just for the unjust –
to bring us to God.

No secondary motive deteriorated the compassion-
ate self-sacrifice of Jesus; yet the denial of himself has
turned to his boundless exaltation. Faith perceives this,
and knowing that in this case one rule holds good for
the Leader and the follower, it accepts all manner of
service, however menial, and it consents with cheerful-
ness to a thorough self-emptying. To lose one's life for
truth's sake and love's sake is to save it according to
biblical philosophy. Mark 8:35 tells us that Jesus said,
*For whosoever will save his life shall lose it; but whoso-
ever shall lose his life for my sake and the gospel's, the
same shall save it.* The complete sinking of self is the
surest road to glory and immortality.

In this way the soul is prepared and rescued from
a passion which is of all things the most weakening to
the force of virtue.

Jesus Never Doubts

The limping of the leader is the lameness of the follower. A grand advantage to the life of faith is that we follow Jesus who never doubted. In the whole story of his life, from his childhood to his death, there is no trace of doubting. All other men – the best, the firmest, the most learned, and the most godly – have had their times of questioning and their dark hours of mistrust, but Jesus is never uncertain, he never even hesitates.

Knowing the Father, being wholly conformed to him, seeking only his glory, and confiding in the eternal power, he never gropes in darkness but goes serenely forward in a calm, unclouded light. In the hour of his enemies' triumph and of his own passion, he is *exceeding sorrowful, even unto death*, but never mistrustful or dubious (Matthew 26:38). In his mind there never lurked the slightest fear as to the ultimate success of his great enterprise, even though all his disciples forsook him and fled.

To the soldier in battle, the confidence of his captain is worth many battalions. Looking up into the calmly resolute and expectant face of the commander-in-chief, the waverer grows steadfast, and even the most confident is reassured. If the Christ had doubted, the common Christian might have despaired; but since he who bore the brunt of the battle never staggered, it is not ours to question. Had doubt been meritorious or useful, Jesus would not have been without it; had it been a sinless infirmity of manhood, Jesus would have suffered it; and had it been a process needed for growth and development, the Firstborn would have become a partaker in it with the rest of the family. Since Jesus did not doubt, we feel no reverence for skepticism; we judge that it is not necessary for a perfect humanity, and we conclude that the less we have to do with it the better. Do you not believe this is so, good brother?

Faith and Its Early Misgivings

Our chronic condition of unbelief ends with our full confidence in God as he is revealed, but flare-ups of that unbelief are apt to come upon us unaware. Are they not the epilepsies of the mind? Belief in the Great Unseen is not natural to the animal part of us, which still craves something for the eyes by way of signs and wonders. It is a common thing for young believers to be weak upon their feet, for even David prayed, *Have mercy upon me, O LORD; for I am weak* (Psalm 6:2).

The strangeness and greatness of his spiritual discoveries may cause this feeling in the spiritual youth; his memory of past sin and his sense of present weakness may cause him to tremble. But let him hold on with a death grip to his faith in God, and the darkness will pass from over his soul. Experience will come to his aid; he will find it easier to trust as belief becomes a habit, and one day he will reach to that triumphant faith of afflicted Job when he said, *Though he slay me, yet I will trust in him* (Job 13:15).

Faith Must Not Be Mixed

There is a tendency among those who are aiming at a noble life to mix up their faith in God with other matters. Anxious to enjoy every aid to faith, they are apt to buttress the Rock of Ages with timber from their own forests. This will prove to be a great source of confusion. If we trust God at all, we must trust him altogether. The Highest Power includes every other, and therefore, the notion of adding anything to the living God is as absurd as it is insulting. Do I trust in God to save me from sin in his own promised way? Then I am to believe that he will accomplish his promise whether I feel better or worse. If it is God who is believed, he cannot alter or falter, and therefore, he should receive the same credit at one time as at another. True, *we* may have seriously declined, but the stress lies upon the faithfulness of God, and until that can be challenged, why should we doubt? *If we are unfaithful, yet he remains faithful; he cannot deny himself* (2 Timothy 2:13).

Imagine that the purpose is to be achieved by two forces; then our confidence in one may vary with the condition of the other. But if the design is in the hands of One Power alone, then a reduction of confidence cannot be justified unless the One Power manifests signs of decay. Faith in God must be unadulterated. Even holy anxiety and watchfulness must not be allowed to shift the ground of our trust. We must lean hard and lean wholly upon Him who is exalted to be a Prince and a Savior, whose work it is to save his people from their sins.

The Believer As a Missionary

He who has believed in Jesus for himself will be hopeful for his friends and brothers. This hopefulness is a great assistance in doing good. Many have failed to save others because they had no faith in the possibility of saving them. A genuine Christian loses hope for no man since he has found grace himself. The Word that had power with his own mind may influence others; hence, he would attempt to convert the Pope or the Grand Turk if he had the opportunity, and failing these, he would set to work upon the first who offered himself. For God *having placed in us the word of reconciliation. Now then we are ambassadors for Christ, as though God did exhort you by us; we beseech you in Christ's name, be ye reconciled to God* (2 Corinthians 5:19-20). A living faith is a propagating faith. If you have no concern for the soul of your neighbor, it is time that you have a fear for your own soul.

Faith, Not Fancy

God is to be trusted for what he is and not for what he is not. We may confidently expect him to act according to his nature, but never contrary to it. To dream that God will do this and that because we wish that he would is not faith but fanaticism. Faith can only stand upon truth. We may be sure that God will act to honor his own justice, mercy, wisdom, and power – in a word, to be himself. Beyond all doubt, he will fulfill his promises, and when faith grasps a promise, she is on sure ground.

To believe that God will give us what he has never promised to give is mere dreaming. Faith without a promise implied or revealed is folly. Though our trust should cry itself hoarse in prayer, it would be nonetheless a vain old simpleton if it had no word of God to warrant it. Happily, the promises and unveilings of Scripture are ample for every real emergency, but when unrestrained credence catches every whim of its own crazy imagination and expects

> **Happily, the promises and unveilings of Scripture are ample for every real emergency.**

answers to be realized, the disappointment should not be a cause for surprise. It is ours to believe the sure things of God's revelation, but we are not to waste a grain of precious reliance upon anything outside of that circle.

Advanced Thought

None of us yet know all that God may teach us from his Word. We have waded into the shallows of that great sea, but oh, the depths! We are to grow in heavenly knowledge. We are told to *grow in grace and in the knowledge of our Lord and Saviour, Jesus Christ* (2 Peter 3:18). Possibly one generation may advance upon another in such knowledge. But some growth is suspicious, especially that which weakens faith. It is certain that from the apostolic period to the Dark

Ages, if the church advanced at all, it was in a backward direction. Religious thought digressed in a wretched fashion away from truth for several centuries. It is more than possible that modern thought is starting on another such digressive period.

Those who are infatuated with novelties may make a dogma out of a certain preacher's statement that "the Lord hath more truth yet to break forth out of His Holy Word."[11] But without denying it, we question the common interpretation of the prophecy. If it meant that apostles, confessors, and martyrs did not know the meaning of God's revelation, that holy men of former years were ignoramuses compared with our present professors, and that Puritans and the like are all to be discarded because new lamps have eclipsed the old light, then we believe the statement to be one great, broad, pestilent lie.

God has not left these nineteen centuries without his grace. He has not tantalized the ages with a Bible that can only be opened by a succession of Germans with big pipes. We have measured the boasters who are the apostles of "modern thought," and we are slow to admit that the truth of the gospel was purposely involved in obscurity that their vast intellects might in due time develop it. Under their management our churches are famishing, and religion is falling into contempt. Yet we must daily wait at the posts of their doors while their changing oracles reveal to us the progressive theology.

Bah! We shall go on feeding men with the bread of

11   John Robinson, phrase from his farewell sermon before the Mayflower sailed.

heaven, while these pretenders are proving that sawdust is the true stuffing for the human doll.

Faith for Every Day

God is one. God's works and ways are one. His laws for earth are in the same statute book as those for heaven. The natural, as God made it, is not in conflict with the spiritual. The line between secular and sacred things is imaginary and mischievous. We believe God for time as well as for eternity, for earth as well as for heaven, for the body as well as for the soul. Far be it for any honest man to confine his faith in God to certain mysterious and indiscernible concerns and doubt him when it comes to his immediate business and the trials of everyday life.

We are taught by our Great Master to pray to the heavenly Father, *Thy kingdom come,* and the same prayer includes the petition, *Give us this day our daily bread* (Matthew 6:10-11). To confide to heaven the greater cares and leave the lesser to unbelief would be as unwise as to commit the door of the house to a watchman but keep an open window from his sight. What is little? What is trifling? There exists no such thing to a wise man anxious to be always right. We are told to *pray without ceasing. In every thing give thanks: for this is the will of God in Christ Jesus concerning you* (1 Thessalonians 5:17-18).

No, we must have a present, house-keeping, shop-keeping, table-furnishing faith, for if our strength is only available on great occasions, we may be utterly undone by the ills to which it is inapplicable. *The just shall live by faith* (Romans 1:17). Faith is not a go-to-meeting coat for us, but an everyday suit. Comprehensive, universal, and constant in operation, it is a principle that those who are perpetually in danger and constantly in need always require. As the cherubic sword turned every way to keep the gate of Eden, so does faith guard the soul from the advance of enemies; let them come from what point of the compass they may.

Faith Works

Sincere faith belongs not to the tribe of *Lazzaroni*.[12] To leave all things to come as they may and attempt nothing is more the accompaniment of despair than of confidence. Convinced of the fertility of the soil, the farmer sows it; assured of victory, the soldier fights for it; relying on his good ship, the mariner puts to sea. We cannot believe in God who works evermore and then work no more. Faith never regards it as advantageous to rust in inglorious rest. No, faith in matters of common life bores the Alps, unites the seas, invades the unknown, and braves the perilous.

When that same principle exercises itself upon God and all his purifying forces, it wrestles with habits, conquers passions, rises to self-denial, and makes a man a hero. When we believe best, we accomplish most. Like the valve that regulates the quantity of steam, so faith, by its decline or advance, increases or decreases the

---

12   In the Age of Revolution, the Lazzaroni were the poorest of the lower class in the city and kingdom of Naples, Italy. They were often depicted as beggars who formed mobs and followed political leaders.

spiritual force which is admitted to the soul from its God. Thus, it becomes most important that we not only have faith, but that we also have it more abundantly. The rule of the kingdom is, *According to your faith be it unto you* (Matthew 9:29).

Faith Waits

Unbelief in the heart must see an effect following a cause in every instance, or else she doubts the cause; faith is in no such hurry. In nature, the more precious operations are slow; the process that produces mushrooms in a night is admirable, but there are nobler things than fungi, and these do not come as suddenly.

To produce a certain condition, preceding phenomena may appear to cause the reverse; a June garden, filled with many colored flowers, is preceded by the clouded, weeping skies of April and the fitful changes of May. What then? Faith accepts the immutability of God's nature and promise as her solace and security against the perpetual changes of outward things. Looking behind the shifting scenery of the visible, she is not perplexed by adverse appearances. God works as he pleases. He does not explain his methods but bids us believe his promises.

The most noxious elements may appear to be cast into the refiner's fire, and the smoke of a furnace may rise in the process, but the highest good is distilled in due time. At no moment in the formation of things would doubt be satisfied, for its criticisms are those of ignorance, but the believing man refrains from judging unfinished work. His eye is prophetic, and he sees the good that will come in the end and therefore plucks no apple until it is ripe. Hurry and worry, fret and sweat, are for short-sighted passion; but rest and quiet, force and prudence, are with strong confidence. *For the LORD shall be thy confidence, and shall keep thy foot from being taken* (Proverbs 3:26).

Faith Sings

Faith's life is song. She marches to battle with a psalm. She suffers with a hymn upon her lips. She glorifies God in the fires. She passes out of the world to the music of the "Te Deum"[13] and not to the mournful notes of a dirge. She thrusts out the wailers and lamenters from the chamber of her departed and enters the room, having none with her but the Lord, who is the Resurrection and the Life. Does doubt compose sonnets or chant hosannas? Can she even write a requiem? Hers are what the Poet calls "bitter notes." Let her go and howl by the Dead Sea over Sodom and Gomorrah!

Faith Magnifies Prayer

The believing man resorts to God at all times so he may keep up his fellowship with the divine mind. Prayer is not a soliloquy, but a dialogue; not an introspection, but a looking towards *the hills, whence cometh my help* (Psalm 121:1). There is a relief in unburdening the mind to a sympathetic friend, and faith feels this abundantly,

---

13   "Te Deum" is a Latin Christian hymn composed in the 4th century, which ends with a selection of verses from the book of Psalms. It follows the outline of the Apostles' Creed with a mixture of a poetic vision of heaven and a declaration of faith.

casting all your cares upon him, for he cares for you (1 Peter 5:7); but there is more than this in prayer. When an obedient activity has worked to exhaustion, but the need is not fulfilled, then the hand of God is trusted in to go beyond, just as it was relied upon before to go with us. Faith has no desire to have its own will when that will is not in accordance with the mind of God, for such a desire would be the impulse of an unbelief that did not rely upon God's judgment as our best guide. Faith knows that God's will is the highest good, and that any petitions which are beneficial to us will be granted. All things are ours already by love's gift, and prayer is the check we use to draw from our own bank account with God. Thus, the believer has a sense of boundless riches without the peril of them.

Faith Enjoys the Eternal Harmonies

Trust in the Great Father suggests and fosters delight in all his works. We are out of gear with the universe until we are at peace with God, and then all the creatures enter into a league of harmony with us and we with them. At home in our Father's house, everything communes with us of his glory. Shrines grow needless, for the whole creation is the work of the Lord, and nothing is any longer common or unclean. Mountains and hills break forth before us into singing, and all the trees of the field do clap their hands. It was no wonder that a great saint called the birds his sisters, for we seem to share in all of our Maker's creation. Instead of being loose stones cast out as useless, we are built into the fabric of the divine Architect and are in accord with all the worlds. No one takes a more intense delight in nature than the intelligent friend of God, who is the world's Interpreter and Voice; its inmost secret is laid bare to him. "Nature is but a name for an effect whose cause is God."[14] He perceives God's hand everywhere, even the God of Gethsemane and the cross.

> One spirit – His
> Who wore the platted thorns with bleeding brows
> Rules universal nature.[15]

The scientist talks of natural laws, and the theologian discusses the Decalogue (Ten Commandments); but to the believer all laws are in one statute book, and he honors all for the King's sake. He sees no holiness within walls superior to that which is outside; every place to him is hallowed, for God is there. The rain is holy water, the mountain basin a baptistery, the flight of birds a sacred procession, the harvest a sacrament, the thunder a hymn, the lightning a sermon. Faith floods the universe with Deity by revealing that unbounded Presence which is evermore its life, its bliss.

A Stay-by

In times of spiritual conflict, when the truth of the

---

14   William Cowper (1731-1800), from *The Task*.
15   Ibid.

gospel has been called into question, we have known a believing man to take his stand at night under the starry vault of heaven, look up, and cry, "My God, I feel an intense love for thee, thy ways, thy laws, thy service! For thou art infinitely good and glorious!" Then he concluded that the gospel, which has brought him into a state of unbounded affection for God, must be true. Unconsciously the mind judges as if it saw an identity between truth and right. This instinct is true. That which makes a man pure must have truth in it; that which defiles him is a lie.

A Further Help

Going to his chamber, the tempted one bowed his knee and prayed out of a full heart for all mankind, heartily desiring their welfare and asking for grace personally to promote it. He petitioned for the forgiveness of all those who without cause have done him wrong. He pleaded against selfishness and every unloving thought. Rising from his knees, he has another weapon at hand against doubt; for the faith which led him into this condition of pure, heartfelt love must be the truth. Though this may not be rational, and the logic of it may not be acceptable to other men, yet we affirm that to that man, it is good evidence and in many ways better than any verbal argument. Love and truth agree in one, and the one works into the hands of the other. Truth begets love, and hatred is born of falsehood.

Gloriously True

If the things that our faith receives are indeed facts, they are tremendously true and demand life at its utmost stretch from us. Revelation does not deal with trifles. Let men take heed how they behave themselves amid eternal truths.

Furthermore, the believer rejoices that these things are also gloriously true. His is an inheritance of inconceivable magnificence. The truths which surround the life of faith are worthy of immortals; yes, worthy of God himself. Let us walk according to our high calling. Oh, for passion fit for the temple of the Infinite, wherein we minister this day!

Faith and the End

The Lord Jesus has promised to come again, and faith clings to this promise. He said, *And if I go and prepare a place for you, I will come again and take you unto myself; that where I am, there ye may be also* (John 14:3). Sometimes faith hopes that it may be so soon fulfilled that death may be avoided, but times and seasons are of small consequence, since all the blessings of the second coming will be hers one way or another.

> The Lord Jesus has promised to come again, and faith clings to this promise.

If the Lord should come speedily so that we do not see death, we shall be changed; and if he delays so that we die, we shall be raised incorruptible. Paul told the Corinthians: *Behold, I show you a mystery:*

We shall all indeed be raised, but we shall not all be changed; in a moment, in the twinkling of an eye, at the last trumpet, for the trumpet shall sound, and the dead shall be raised without corruption, and we shall be changed (1 Corinthians 15:51-52). In any case, we shall be forever with him. Wherefore whether we sleep or wake is a matter about which we do not worry. The believer said, *For to me to live is Christ and to die is gain* (Philippians 1:21). How slight the difference!

Finally

We have never seen a dying man repent of his faith in God or of the life which has grown out of it. Deathbeds have been clouded with myriads of regrets, but no one has ever bemoaned his too-early, or too-complete, or too-continuous confidence in God. What no man has regretted let all men pursue.

Fathers and grandfathers have passed this way before us and have entreated us to follow them: they loved us too well to have implored us to trust in Jesus if he had proved to be a vain confidence. Their dying testimony commands our reverent obedience. *Therefore, seeing we also are compassed about with so great a cloud of witnesses, leaving behind all the weight of the sin which surrounds us, let us run with patience the race that is set before us, with our eyes fixed on Jesus, the author and finisher of our faith, who having been offered joy, endured the cross[a], despising the shame and was seated at the right hand of the throne of God* (Hebrews 12:1-2).

Thus, let time and eternity bring what they may, we commit ourselves unto God as unto a faithful Creator.

To whom be glory
for ever and ever.
Amen.

Charles H. Spurgeon – A Brief Biography

Charles Haddon Spurgeon was born on June 19, 1834, in Kelvedon, Essex, England. He was one of seventeen children in his family (nine of whom died in infancy). His father and grandfather were Nonconformist ministers in England. Due to economic difficulties, eighteen-month-old Charles was sent to live with his grandfather, who helped teach Charles the ways of God. Later in life, Charles remembered looking at the pictures in *Pilgrim's Progress* and in *Foxe's Book of Martyrs* as a young boy.

Charles did not have much of a formal education and never went to college. He read much throughout his life though, especially books by Puritan authors.

Even with godly parents and grandparents, young Charles resisted giving in to God. It was not until he was fifteen years old that he was born again. He was on his way to his usual church, but when a heavy snowstorm prevented him from getting there, he turned in at a little Primitive Methodist chapel. Though there were only about fifteen people in attendance, the preacher spoke from Isaiah 45:22: *Look unto me, and be ye saved, all the ends of the earth.* Charles Spurgeon's eyes were opened and the Lord converted his soul.

He began attending a Baptist church and teaching Sunday school. He soon preached his first sermon, and then when he was sixteen years old, he became the pastor of a small Baptist church in Cambridge. The church soon grew to over four hundred people, and Charles Spurgeon, at the age of nineteen, moved on to become the pastor of the New Park Street Church in London. The church grew from a few hundred attenders to a few thousand. They built an addition to the church, but still needed more room to accommodate the congregation. The Metropolitan Tabernacle was built in London in 1861, seating more than 5,000 people. Pastor Spurgeon preached the simple message of the cross, and thereby attracted many people who wanted to hear God's Word preached in the power of the Holy Spirit.

On January 9, 1856, Charles married Susannah Thompson. They had twin boys, Charles and Thomas.

Charles and Susannah loved each other deeply, even amidst the difficulties and troubles that they faced in life, including health problems. They helped each other spiritually, and often together read the writings of Jonathan Edwards, Richard Baxter, and other Puritan writers.

Charles Spurgeon was a friend of all Christians, but he stood firmly on the Scriptures, and it didn't please all who heard him. Spurgeon believed in and preached on the sovereignty of God, heaven and hell, repentance, revival, holiness, salvation through Jesus Christ alone, and the infallibility and necessity of the Word of God. He spoke against worldliness and hypocrisy among Christians, and against Roman Catholicism, ritualism, and modernism.

One of the biggest controversies in his life was known as the "Down-Grade Controversy." Charles Spurgeon believed that some pastors of his time were "downgrading" the faith by compromising with the world or the new ideas of the age. He said that some pastors were denying the inspiration of the Bible, salvation by faith alone, and the truth of the Bible in other areas, such as creation. Many pastors who believed what Spurgeon condemned were not happy about this, and Spurgeon eventually resigned from the Baptist Union.

Despite some difficulties, Spurgeon became known as the "Prince of Preachers." He opposed slavery, started a pastors' college, opened an orphanage, led in helping feed and clothe the poor, had a book fund for pastors who could not afford books, and more.

Charles Spurgeon remains one of the most published preachers in history. His sermons were printed each week (even in the newspapers), and then the sermons for the year were re-issued as a book at the end of the year. The first six volumes, from 1855-1860, are known as *The Park Street Pulpit*, while the next fifty-seven volumes, from 1861-1917 (his sermons continued to be published long after his death), are known as *The Metropolitan Tabernacle Pulpit*. He also oversaw a monthly magazine-type publication called *The Sword and the Trowel,* and Spurgeon wrote many books, including *Lectures to My Students*, *All of Grace*, *Around the Wicket Gate*, *Advice for Seekers*, *John Ploughman's Talks*, *The Soul Winner*, *Words of Counsel for Christian Workers*, *Cheque Book of the Bank of Faith*, *Morning and Evening*, his autobiography, and more, including some commentaries, such as his twenty-year study on the Psalms – *The Treasury of David*.

Charles Spurgeon often preached ten times a week, preaching to an estimated ten million people during his lifetime. He usually preached from only one page of notes, and often from just an outline. He read about six books each week. During his lifetime, he had read *The Pilgrim's Progress* through more than one hundred times. When he died, his personal library consisted of more than 12,000 books. However, the Bible always remained the most important book to him.

Spurgeon was able to do what he did in the power of God's Holy Spirit because he followed his own advice – he met with God every morning before meeting with others, and he continued in communion with God throughout the day.

Charles Spurgeon suffered from gout, rheumatism, and some depression, among other health problems. He often went to Menton, France, to recuperate and rest. He preached his final sermon at the Metropolitan Tabernacle on June 7, 1891, and died in France on January 31, 1892, at the age of fifty-seven. He was buried in Norwood Cemetery in London.

Charles Haddon Spurgeon lived a life devoted to God. His sermons and writings continue to influence Christians all over the world.

Other Similar Titles

Words of Warning,
by Charles H. Spurgeon

This book, *Words of Warning*, is an analysis of people and the gospel of Christ. Under inspiration of the Holy Spirit, Charles H. Spurgeon sheds light on the many ways people may refuse to come to Christ, but he also shines a brilliant light on how we can be saved. Unsaved or wavering individuals will be convicted, and if they allow it, they will be led to Christ. Sincere Christians will be happy and blessed as they consider the great salvation with which they have been saved.

Available where books are sold.

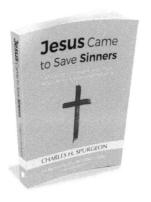

Jesus Came to Save Sinners,
by Charles H. Spurgeon

This is a heart-level conversation with you, the reader. Every excuse, reason, and roadblock for not coming to Christ is examined and duly dealt with. If you think you may be too bad, or if perhaps you really are bad and you sin either openly or behind closed doors, you will discover that life in Christ is for you too. You can reject the message of salvation by faith, or you can choose to live a life of sin after professing faith in Christ, but you cannot change the truth as it is, either for yourself or for others. As such, it behooves you and your family to embrace truth, claim it for your own, and be genuinely set free for now and eternity. Come and embrace this free gift of God, and live a victorious life for Him.

Available where books are sold.

According to Promise,
by Charles H. Spurgeon

The first part of this book is meant to be a sieve to separate the chaff from the wheat. Use it on your own soul. It may be the most profitable and beneficial work you have ever done. He who looked into his accounts and found that his business was losing money was saved from bankruptcy. This may happen also to you. If, however, you discover that your heavenly business is prospering, it will be a great comfort to you. You cannot lose by honestly searching your own heart.

The second part of this book examines God's promises to His children. The promises of God not only exceed all precedent, but they also exceed all imitation. No one has been able to compete with God in the language of liberality. The promises of God are as much above all other promises as the heavens are above the earth.

Available where books are sold.

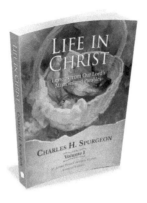

Life in Christ (Vol. 1),
by Charles H. Spurgeon

Men who were led by the hand or groped their way along the wall to reach Jesus were touched by his finger and went home without a guide, rejoicing that Jesus Christ had opened their eyes. Jesus is still able to perform such miracles. And, with the power of the Holy Spirit, his Word will be expounded and we'll watch for the signs to follow, expecting to see them at once. Why shouldn't those who read this be blessed with the light of heaven? This is my heart's inmost desire.

I can't put fine words together. I've never studied speech. In fact, my heart loathes the very thought of intentionally speaking with fine words when souls are in danger of eternal separation from God. No, I work to speak straight to your hearts and consciences, and if there is anyone with faith to receive, God will bless them with fresh revelation.

– Charles H. Spurgeon

Available where books are sold.

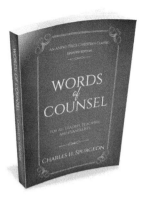

Words of Counsel, by Charles H. Spurgeon

Is there any occupation as profitable or rewarding as that of winning souls for Christ? It is a desirable employment, and the threshold for entry into this profession is set at a level any Christian may achieve – you must only love the Lord God with all your heart, soul, and mind; and your fellow man as yourself. This work is for all genuine Christians, of all walks of life. This is for you, fellow Christian.

Be prepared to be inspired, challenged, and convicted. Be prepared to weep, for the Holy Spirit may touch you deeply as you consider your coworkers, your neighbors, the children you know, and how much the Lord cares for these individuals. But you will also be equipped. Charles Spurgeon knew something about winning souls, and he holds nothing back as he shares biblical wisdom and practical application regarding the incredible work the Lord wants to do through His people to reach the lost.

Available where books are sold.

The Soul Winner, by Charles H. Spurgeon

As an individual, you may ask, How can I, an average person, do anything to reach the lost? Or if a pastor, you may be discouraged and feel ineffective with your congregation, much less the world. Or perhaps you don't yet have a heart for the lost. Whatever your excuse, it's time to change. Overcome yourself and learn to make a difference in your church and the world around you. It's time to become an effective soul winner for Christ.

As Christians, our main business is to win souls. But, in Spurgeon's own words, "like shoeing-smiths, we need to know a great many things. Just as the smith must know about horses and how to make shoes for them, so we must know about souls and how to win them for Christ." Learn about souls, and how to win them, from one of the most acclaimed soul winners of all time.

Available where books are sold.

The Greatest Fight,
by Charles H. Spurgeon

This book examines three things that are of utmost importance in this fight of faith. The first is *our armory*, which is the inspired Word of God. The second is *our army*, the church of the living God, which we must lead under our Lord's command. The third is *our strength*, by which we wear the armor and use the sword.

The message in this book, when originally presented by Charles Spurgeon in his final address to his own Pastor's College, was received rapturously and enthusiastically. It was almost immediately published and distributed around the world and in several languages. After Charles Spurgeon's death in 1892, 34,000 copies were printed and distributed to pastors and leaders in England through Mrs. Spurgeon's book fund. It is with great pleasure that we present this updated and very relevant book to the Lord's army of today.

Available where books are sold.

Come Ye Children, by Charles H. Spurgeon

Teaching children things of the Lord is an honor and a high calling. Children have boundless energy and may appear distracted, but they are capable of understanding biblical truths even adults have a hard time grasping. Children's minds are easily impressed with new thoughts, whether good or bad, and will remember many of their young lessons for the rest of their life. Adults and churches tend to provide entertainment to occupy the children, but children ought to have our undivided attention. Jesus said, let the little children come to me. They were worthy of His time and devotion, and they are worthy of ours.

Available where books are sold.

Following Christ, by Charles H. Spurgeon

You cannot have Christ if you will not serve Him. If you take Christ, you must take Him in all His qualities. You must not simply take Him as a Friend, but you must also take Him as your Master. If you are to become His disciple, you must also become His servant. God-forbid that anyone fights against that truth. It is certainly one of our greatest delights on earth to serve our Lord, and this is to be our joyful vocation even in heaven itself: *His servants shall serve Him: and they shall see His face* (Revelation 22:3-4).

Available where books are sold.

CPSIA information can be obtained
at www.ICGtesting.com
Printed in the USA
LVHW080930010222
709923LV00023B/708

9 781622 456253